SOCIAL SCIENCE
PRIMARY 5

BY ME

ACTIVITY BOOK

UNIT 1 The Universe

1 Complete the text about stars.

temperature	Earth	reactions	distance	colour
sizes	Sun	light	gas	enormous

The __________ is the closest star to the Earth. Stars are enormous spheres of __________ where nuclear reactions take place. These __________ produce light and heat. Stars are classified according to three characteristics: __________, size and luminosity. Stars can be blue, yellow, orange, red or white. A star's colour depends on its __________.

Stars can be many different __________. Very small stars are called white dwarves and __________ stars are called red giants. The Sun is an average-sized star. Its diameter is 100 times the Earth's diameter. Red giants, however, can have a diameter up to 500 times that of the Sun.

Luminosity is the amount of __________ from a star that reaches the __________. Luminosity depends on a star's size, temperature and its __________ from Earth.

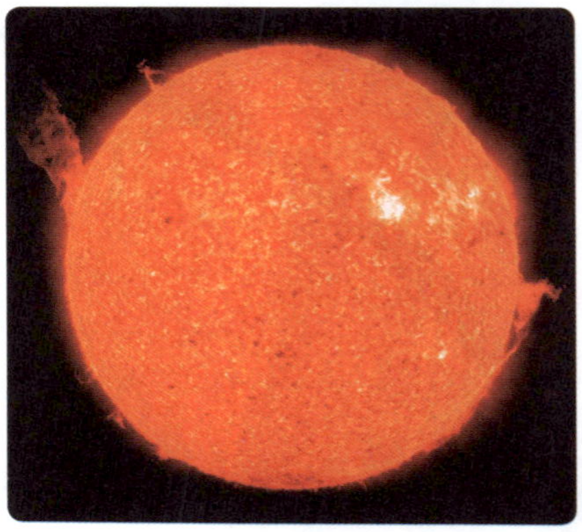

2 Complete the diagram with the information about comets and asteroids.

orbit the Sun	are made of rock	are made of ice, gas and dust	have a bright tail
are part of the Solar System	have no tail	orbit in the Kuiper Belt	have a coma and a nucleus

comets

asteroids

3 Match the definitions with the words.

a. These are formed when they enter the Earth's atmosphere and burn.

b. This is a group of galaxies.

c. These are pieces of a meteoroid that hit Earth.

d. This was a huge explosion that probably marked the beginning of the Universe.

e. These are pieces of rock or metal which form when asteroids collide or break up.

f. This is the largest planet in the Solar System.

1. Big Bang
2. meteroids
3. galaxy cluster
4. meteors
5. meteorites
6. Jupiter

4 Read the text and answer the questions.

If, in the future, astronauts stay on the Moon for long periods of time, they will have to be able to produce their own food. NASA scientists recently announced plans to test growing a vegetable garden on the lunar surface. Of course, this won't be a garden like here on Earth. The astronauts won't plant the seeds on the Moon's surface and hope that they grow.

The seeds will be inside special boxes called Lunar Plant Growth Chambers. The chambers will contain the nutrients that the plant needs, as well as water and air. They will also protect the seeds against solar radiation. Once the garden lands on the Moon, more water will be added. The scientists will study the germination of the seeds. Plants have already been grown on the International Space Station, but this will be the first experiment performed on another world.

a. Where will the plants grow? ____________________

b. What do the special chambers contain? ____________________

c. Do you think that NASA will ever succeed in growing a vegetable garden on the Moon? Why? ____________________

5 Label the celestial bodies in the Solar System.

6 Read and match the headings to the paragraphs. Identify the planet.

Atmosphere and temperature
Distance from the Sun
Other information
Appearance
Size and rotation

______

This planet is the second biggest planet in the Solar System. It has a diameter of approximately 120 000 km. This is more than nine times bigger than the Earth. However, it only takes about 11 hours to complete a full rotation. The Earth takes 24 hours.

______

It has a yellow-coloured surface and there are many beautiful rings orbiting it. These rings are made up of ice and rock particles. There are also more than 50 moons orbiting the planet.

______

It is the sixth planet from the Sun. It is 1.4 billion kilometres from the Sun and its orbit takes about 29 Earth years.

______

It's the least dense planet in the Solar System and it doesn't have a solid surface. It's made up mostly of hydrogen and helium. The average temperature is –185 °C and there are very strong winds.

______

If we could put the planet in a bucket of water, it would float.

7. Read the sentences and decide if they refer to the Earth (E), the Moon (M) or both (B).

a. It has two types of motion: rotation and revolution. ☐

b. It is surrounded by a mixture of gases which make up the atmosphere. ☐

c. Its landscape has craters and mountain ranges. ☐

d. It can't support life. ☐

e. It receives light from the Sun. ☐

f. Its gravity pulls at ocean water and creates tides. ☐

g. It takes 24 hours to complete one rotation. ☐

h. It takes 28 days to complete one revolution. ☐

8. The Earth has two types of motion: rotation and revolution. Read the sentences and identify the movement. Label the photo.

a. The Earth spins on its axis. ____________

b. It takes 365 days. ____________

c. The Earth orbits the Sun. ____________

d. It takes 24 hours. ____________

e. This movement gives us night. ____________

f. This movement gives us seasons. ____________

____

9. Label the phases of the Moon.

a  ____________

b  ____________

c  ____________

d  ____________

Project work

10 Choose two planets and find out more about them. Complete the index cards. Draw the planet and its moons.

Planet name: __________

It is the __________ planet from the Sun.

Number of moons: __________

Surface temperature: __________

Made up of: __________

Time for one orbit: __________

Planet name: __________

It is the __________ planet from the Sun.

Number of moons: __________

Surface temperature: __________

Made up of: __________

Time for one orbit: __________

11 Analyse the information from Activity 10 and answer the questions.

a. Which planet is closer to the Sun? __________

b. Which planet is hotter? __________

c. Which planet has more moons? __________

d. Which planet orbits quicker? __________

12 Use the information from your index cards to write a short description of one of your chosen planets.

__________ is the __________ from the Sun. It has __________

____

____

Skills check

13 Read the text. Choose the best word for each space.

An astronaut sometimes goes outside the space station to check and repair things. When this happens, the astronaut needs to wear a special (1) ____________ to stay alive. There is no (2) ____________ in space so a special machine on the astronaut's back provides oxygen to breathe and removes carbon dioxide. Astronauts also need protection against the extreme (3) ____________ in space. There is a special item of clothing under the spacesuit which contains tubes of water. Astronauts can fill the tubes with hot water to warm themselves up or cold water to cool down.

A space station orbits the Earth, so it travels through sunlight and darkness. A reflective visor on the (4) ____________ protects the astronaut's eyes from the Sun and special lights help to see in the dark. Finally, there are (5) ____________ at the back of the spacesuit so an astronaut can fly back to the space station if contact is broken.

1. spacesuit / clothes / spacesuits
2. water / air / food
3. wind / temperatures / heat
4. hat / scarf / helmet
5. jets / wheels / wings

14 Complete the definitions.

a. This person is trained to travel in space: ____________

b. This is the Earth's only natural satellite: ____________

c. This is a building with a curved ceiling where the images of various celestial bodies are shown: ____________

d. This is an elliptical path around stars or planets through which celestial bodies move: ____________

15 Explain why the following names are important.

a. Yuri Gagarin *was the first human to walk on the Moon.*

b. Neil Armstrong ____________

c. Apollo 11 ____________

d. Voyager 1 and Voyager 2 ____________

e. Salyut 1 ____________

UNIT 2 Representing the Earth

1 Which symbol would you look for if you wanted to do these things?

a. park your car ☐

b. get information about the city you're in ☐

c. see a doctor ☐

d. take a taxi ☐

e. send a letter ☐

f. go shopping ☐

g. stay in a campsite ☐

h. visit a museum ☐

i. worship ☐

j. attend a university lecture ☐

2 Look at the map. Start from the X and follow the directions. Where are you?

a. Cross to the other side of the river. Go past the university and it's on the second street on your left. ____________

b. You'll find it on Main Street, about one block before the shopping centre. ____________

c. Head out towards the airport and you'll see it to your left. ____________

d. There are a couple of them. One's in front of the train station and the other is opposite the hospital. ____________

3 Classify the words according to the sphere of the Earth they belong to.

fish	carbon dioxide	glacier	gas	people	river	snow	soil
plants	oxygen	nitrogen	mountain	clouds	rocks	insects	minerals

hydrosphere	atmosphere	geosphere	biosphere

4 Complete the sentences about the spheres of the Earth.

a. Living things make up the ________________.

b. ________________ makes up the biggest percentage of the atmosphere.

c. The ________________, the ________________ and the core are parts of the Earth's geosphere.

d. The outer core is made of very hot ________________.

5 Write the names of the countries and their capital cities.

1. *France; Paris*
2. ________________
3. ________________
4. ________________
5. ________________
6. ________________
7. ________________
8. ________________

6 Read the text about maps and circle the correct words.

Geographic maps are divided up by lines running north to south and east to west. The *vertical / horizontal* lines are called parallels, while the lines showing *longitude / latitude* are called *meridians / coordinates*. Maps have a *rose / scale* to express the difference between actual distances on the Earth and distances on the map. However, maps are *more / less* accurate than globes because they're two-dimensional. To learn where rivers and mountains are, you need a *physical / political* map. There are many different types of maps showing things like climate, population, or even where fish are!

Whatever the map is used for, the person who creates them is called a *geographer / cartographer*.

7 Look at the map and answer the questions.

1. Which continents do these regions belong to?

a. Great Lakes ____________________

b. Tibetan Plateau ____________________

c. Rocky Mountains ____________________

d. Atlas Mountains ____________________

e. The Andes ____________________

f. Lake Baikal ____________________

g. Kalahari Desert ____________________

2. Give one example of each landform.

a. mountains ____________________

b. plateau ____________________

c. lake ____________________

d. desert ____________________

e. sea ____________________

f. cape ____________________

3. Which oceans do these seas belong to?

a. Coral Sea ____________________

b. North Sea ____________________

c. Beaufort Sea ____________________

d. Arabian Sea ____________________

e. Caribbean Sea ____________________

f. Tasman Sea ____________________

8 Read the weather forecast and label the map. Write the letter of the weather symbols in the correct places. Draw arrows to show wind speed and direction.

Temperatures in southern Italy will be in the mid-thirties with no chance of rain, but the north can expect showers throughout the day. Germany is experiencing light winds from the west with a chance of rain by the evening. Spain's drought continues, with thunder and lightning expected on the southeastern coast in the afternoon. There will be light to moderate easterly winds throughout the Mediterranean. Summer hasn't yet arrived in the UK. The north of Scotland started out foggy this morning and the southern regions are looking cloudy with sunny periods later on. England will suffer torrential rain all day with high winds from the north.

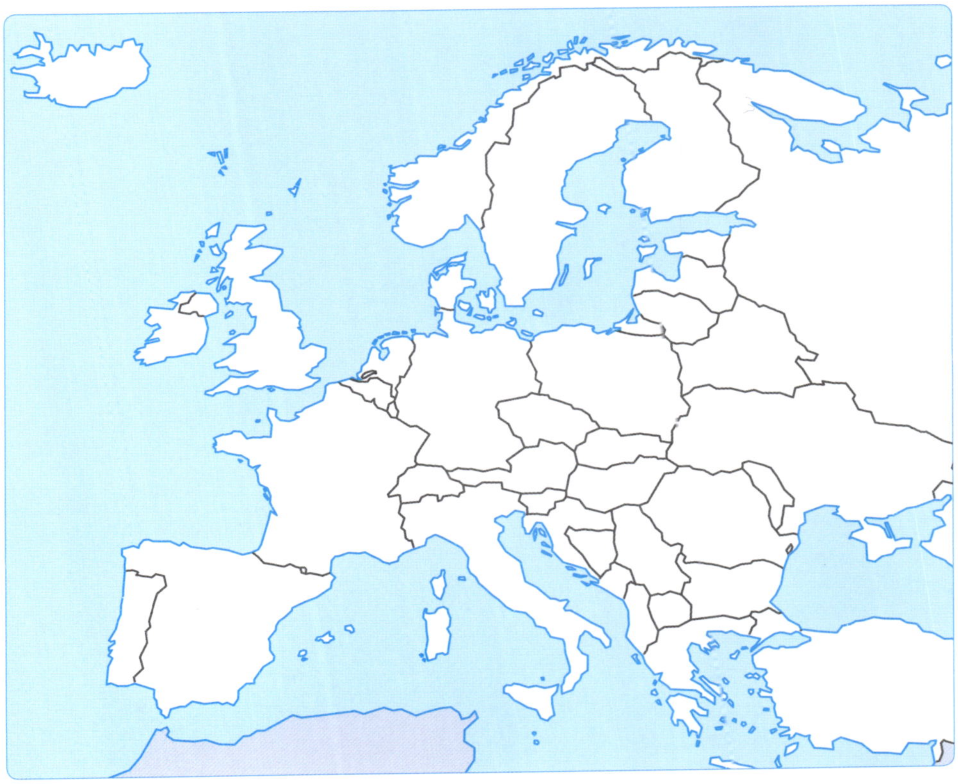

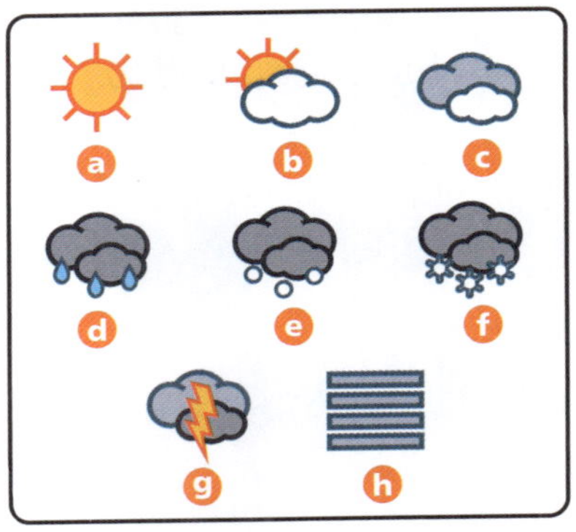

9 Complete the sentences about GPS.

a. GPS stands for ______________________________________

____.

b. Most people use GPS in ______________________________.

c. GPS works by sending ______________________ from satellites.

d. There are ______________ satellites positioned around the Earth.

e. GPS is used by environmental scientists to monitor natural and man-made disasters such as ______________________________.

Project work

10 Early cartographers drew maps without the help of photos or satellites. Think about your town or city and try to draw a map of it in the box below. Include its borders and any geographical features.

11 Now make a key for your map. Include all the symbols that you have used and explain them.

12 If you had been a cartographer 300 years ago, would it have been easier or more difficult to draw a map of your city? Why or why not?

Skills check

13. Read the email and choose the best word for each space.

Hi!

I'm visiting Spain next week (1) ____________ my family.
I would love (2) ____________ see you while we're in Barcelona.
We arrive (3) ____________ Saturday morning (4) ____________
9 am. Why don't we all go (5) ____________ lunch? Where would
be an easy place (6) ____________ meet?

Love,

Maria

1. to / with / for
2. in / to / from
3. in / on / at
4. at / in
5. to / for / from
6. for / from / to

14. Read the email again and answer the questions.

a. Is this email formal or informal? ____________

b. How do you start emails to friends? ____________

c. How do you finish them? ____________

d. Can you use contractions? ____________

15. Write a short email.

A friend and their family are visiting you in your town for the first time next week. You need to arrange a place to meet them. Write an email to your friend. In your email, you should:

- suggest a place and time to meet
- give directions how to get there
- tell them what to do if they're late/lost

Dear ____________

UNIT 3 Climate and weather

1 Read the sentences. What do they describe? Write **W** for weather or **C** for climate.

a. It's raining outside. ☐

b. There's low precipitation all year. ☐

c. It's hot and humid in the summer. ☐

d. It's hotter than yesterday. ☐

e. It's cloudy today. ☐

f. There's a long dry season. ☐

g. It's always cold in winter. ☐

h. I think there's going to be a storm. ☐

2 Complete the sentences about the factors that influence climate.

a. Latitude measures the d____________ from the Equator. It affects the t____________ of a place.

b. Altitude measures the h____________ above sea level of a given area. It affects the t____________ and the amount of precipitacion.

c. The d____________ from the sea affects the temperature of a place; temperatures near the sea are usually c____________ in summer and w____________ in winter when compared to inland areas.

d. High l____________ near the coast affect inland temperature because they prevent the cool sea air from reaching inland areas.

3 Choose the odd one out.

a. temperature / °C / thermometer / wind / heat

b. barometer / humidity / atmospheric pressure / hPa

c. % / humidity / water / barometer / hygrometer

d. wind / air / hPa / anemometer / km/h

e. precipitation / water / rain gauge / mm / %

④ Analyse the map and complete the key.

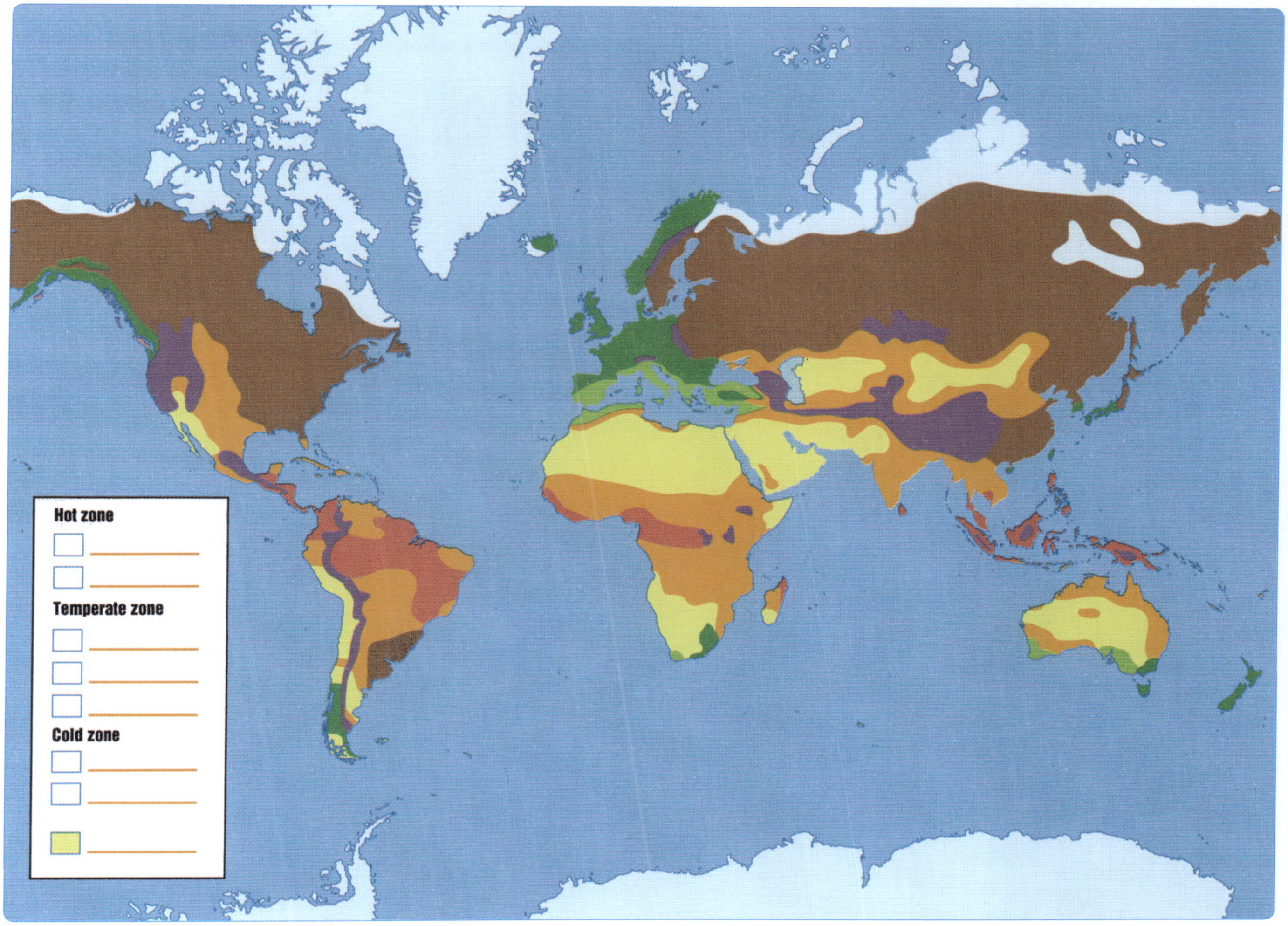

⑤ Complete the sentences about the climate zones.

a. Regions with a ______________ climate have hot summers, cold winters and little rain.

b. The North and South Poles have a ______________ climate.

c. High-altitude regions have a cold, ______________ climate.

d. Coastal regions have a wet, ______________ climate.

e. Regions surrounding the Mediterranean Sea have a ______________ climate.

f. The ______________ climate is found in all three of the climate zones.

6 Label the map. Then classify the cities according to the climate zones they belong to.

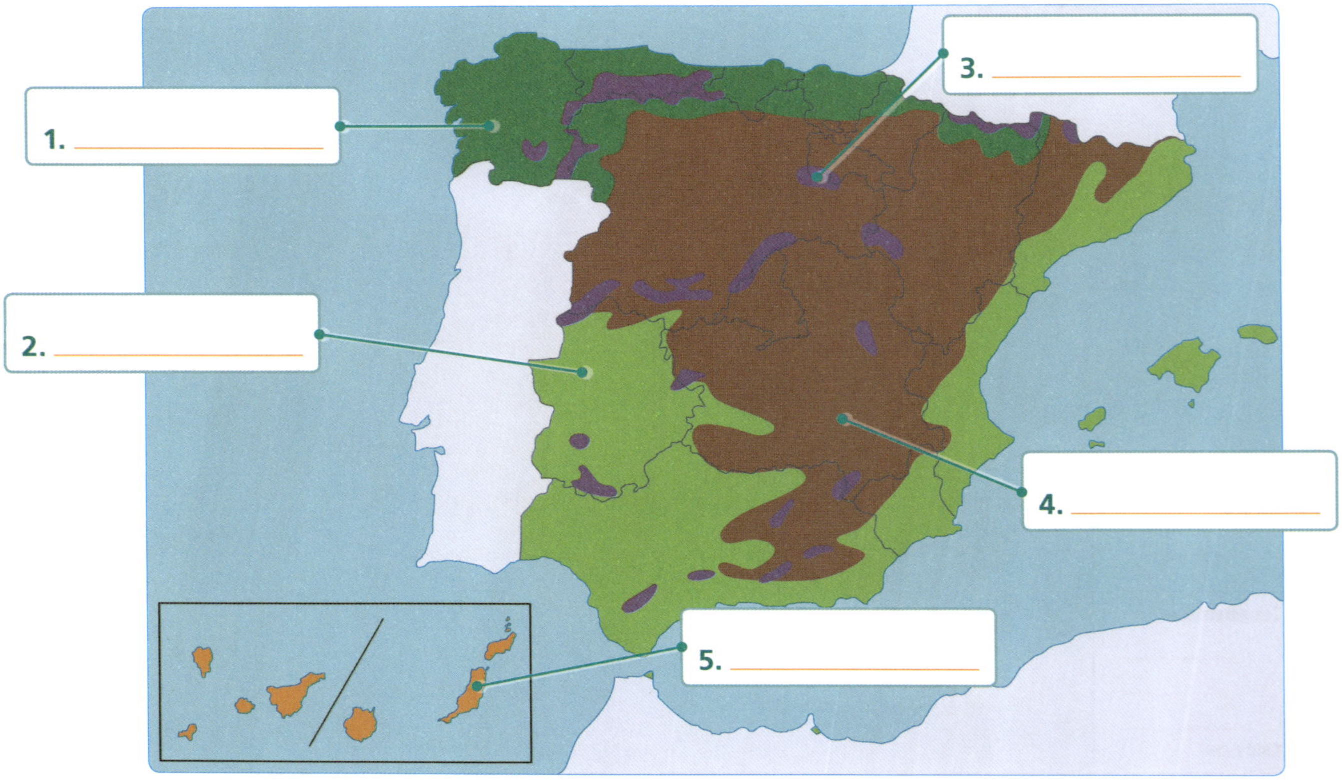

a. Gijón ______

b. Arrecife ______

c. Ceuta ______

d. Albacete ______

7 Complete the text about Bilbao. Write about Cuenca and Huelva. Which city can you see in the photo?

a. Bilbao is on the north coast of Spain and has an ______ climate. It has moderate ______ and high ______. The summers are ______ and the ______ are cool.

b. Cuenca ______

______

______

c. Huelva ______

______

______

______

8 Identify the flora and fauna in the photos. Which climate zones do they belong to?

a

Coniferous trees and the chamois are found in an alpine climate zone.

b

____

____

____

c

____

____

____

9 Complete the text about global warming. There are two extra words.

greenhouse effect	gases	balance	atmosphere	Sun
carbon dioxide	cool down	glaciers	warmer	

The ____________ is the main source of heat on Earth. Gases in the ____________ trap this heat, like the glass in a greenhouse. This is called the ____________. Greenhouse gases, however, aren't necessarily bad. Without any greenhouse gases, too much heat would escape and the Earth would ____________. On the other hand, we know that an excess of greenhouse gases causes global warming. Unfortunately, we are producing large quantities of greenhouse gases, especially ____________. As a result, the Earth is getting ____________ and the polar ice caps and ____________ are melting.

Project work

10 Find out more about the climate zone you live in. Describe the precipitation, tempertatures, and flora and fauna.

I live in ____________. It is in the ____________ of Spain. It has a ____________ climate.

____

____

____

____

11 Search for the information about the average temperatures and precipitation in your region. Complete the climate graph.

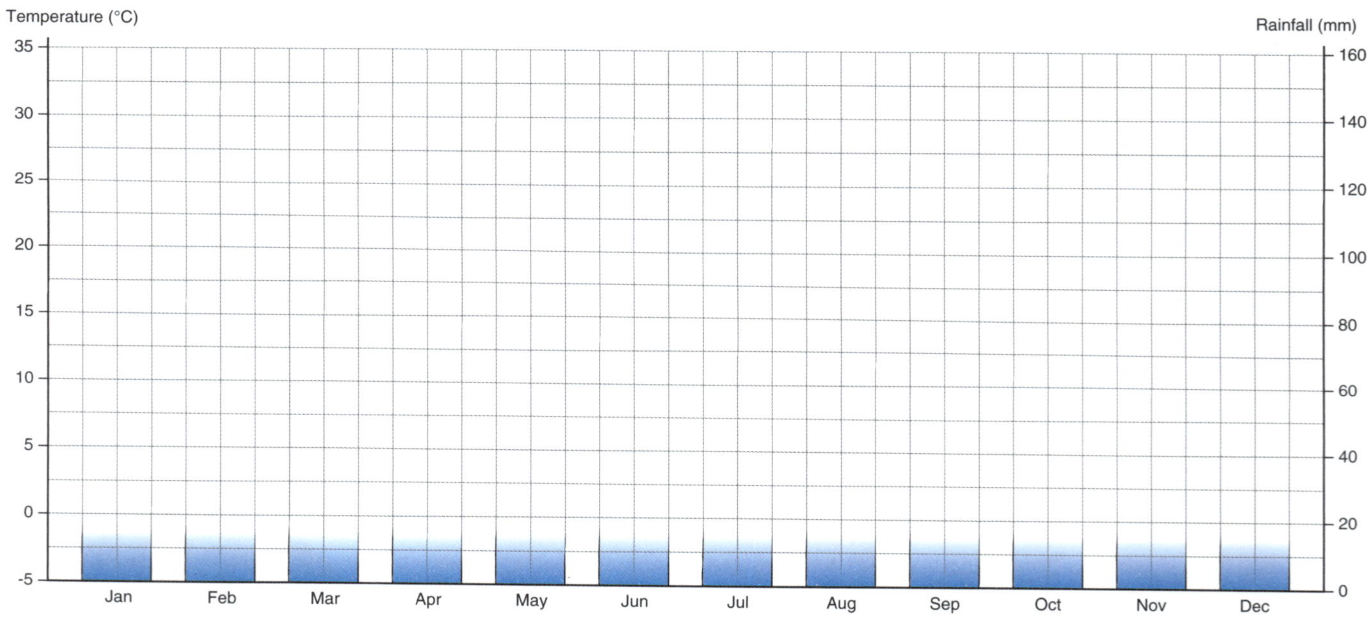

12 Analyse the climate graph from Activity 11 and answer the questions.

a. Which is the hottest month? ____________

b. Which is the coldest month? ____________

c. Which month has the most rain? ____________

d. Which month has the least rain? ____________

e. Which climate zone does your graph represent? ____________

Skills check

13 Match the sentences with the corresponding warning signs. There are four extra sentences.

a. You shouldn't enter this road when it rains heavily.

b. Strong winds will blow before 14 December.

c. You can speed up on the bridge.

d. You shouldn't continue driving because the road is closed.

e. You mustn't swim here.

f. You can park here if there is no snow.

g. You shouldn't drive fast on the bridge.

h. It will be windy on 15 December.

i. You can park here if there is more than 5 centimetres of snow.

j. Visibility might be reduced on the road.

☐ Road may flood

☐ CAUTION! FOG AREA

☐ STRONG WINDS 14-16 DECEMBER

☐ Warning! Do not enter the water

☐ WATCH FOR ICE ON BRIDGE

☐ No parking when snow is over 5 cm

14 Read the texts about extreme weather conditions. Label the photo. Then decide if the problems listed below refer to floods (**F**) or drought (**D**).

Drought occurs when there is little or no precipitation for a long time. Water on land evaporates; rivers and lakes can dry up and disappear. The soil also changes, becoming hard and compact, which means that water can't be absorbed quickly. When precipitation is very heavy or occurs over a long period of time, the water collects on the surface of the Earth and forms a flood. Flooding can also happen when temperatures rise and the snow and ice melts, causing rivers to overflow.

____

a. The soil dries up and becomes cracked. ☐

b. Fresh water supplies become contaminated. ☐

c. Land becomes infertile because it loses its nutrients. ☐

d. Property is damaged and people become homeless. ☐

e. Animals die because they have no water and also because there are no plants to eat. ☐

UNIT 4 Spain's politics and culture

1 Match the terms with the definitions.

a. democracy	**1.** A government with a king or queen at the top.
b. heritage	**2.** Treating someone differently or unfairly because of the group they belong to.
c. constitution	**3.** A system of government where everyone is equal and can elect the political party that will govern.
d. parliament	**4.** Things that people legally and morally have.
e. monarchy	**5.** The fundamental laws of a country.
f. rights	**6.** The group of representatives that rules the country.
g. discrimination	**7.** Traditions that have been passed down from older generations.

2 Answer the questions about the flags of the Autonomous Communities of Spain. If necessary, search for information on the Internet.

a. Which flag has seven stars? What do they represent? ______

b. Which flags feature the Crown of Aragón? ______

c. Which flag has Greek symbols on it? Which symbols? ______

d. Which flags feature a castle or towers? ______

3 Find out more about the food of some of the different regions in Spain.

region	produce	dishes/drinks	festivals
Valencia	*rice*	*paella, horchata*	
Castilla-La Mancha			
Asturias			

4 Which regions are these festival held in? Label the map.

Las Fallas
Feria de Abril
Romería de Andújar
Cruces de Mayo
San Isidro
Sanfermines
La Merced
La Tomatina
Feria del Caballo
Fiesta de los Patios

1. ______________________
2. ______________________
3. ______________________
4. ______________________
5. ______________________
6. ______________________
7. ______________________
8. ______________________

5 Choose a country you would like to know more about. Find out about its festivals and note down what you have learnt in the table.

country: ______________			
festival	city/region	date	celebrations

6 Identify these Spanish UNESCO sites. If necessary, search for the information on the Internet.

a

____

____

b

____

____

c

____

____

7 Complete the text using the words from the box. There are four extra words.

44	China	world	Italy	Europe
Australia	12	buildings	forests	country

Spain has the third highest number of World Heritage sites in the world. Only ______________ and ______________ have more. Of Spain's ______________ sites, 39 are cultural, 3 are natural and 2 are mixed.

One of the newest additions to the list were the mercury mines of Almadén, Castilla-La Mancha. Mercury trade between ______________ and America has been important for centuries, so UNESCO believes it is in the interest of the international community to preserve this area. The mines, and the surrounding ______________, such as Retamar Castle, share their UNESCO status with Idrija in Slovenia. Together, they represent the two largest mercury mines in the ______________.

8 Answer the questions.

a. What is mercury used for? ______________

b. What other things did Spain trade with America in the last few centuries? ______________

c. Would you like to nominate a new site to UNESCO? Which one? Why? ______________

9 Decide if the following words refer to legislative (**L**), executive (**E**) or judicial (**J**) power.

1. judges ☐
2. Senate ☐
3. ministers ☐
4. Government ☐
5. Prime Minister ☐
6. deputies ☐
7. Minister of Education ☐
8. sentences ☐
9. senators ☐
10. Congress ☐
11. magistrates ☐
12. Parliament ☐

10 Now organise the words from Activity 9 in the diagram. Add more words.

Three ____________

- **legislative**
  - ____________
    - ____________ / ____________
    - ____________ / ____________
- **executive**
  - ____________
    - *Prime Minister* / ____________ / ____________
- ____________
  - courts
    - ____________ / ____________ / ____________

11 Answer the questions.

a. Who is the Spanish Head of State? ____________

b. When was the Constitution approved? ____________

c. What is the Spanish national anthem called? ____________

d. How many Autonomous Communities is Spain divided into?

____

e. Which house of the Spanish Parliament is illustrated in the photo?

____

Project work

12 Write a Constitution for your class. First, in groups, write a list of rules that must be followed at school and in the class. Then write a list of the rights and responsibilities for students and teachers.

school rules

- ____________________
- ____________________
- ____________________

Useful language

- You *have to / are required to / must / should ...*
- You *can't / aren't allowed to / mustn't / shouldn't ...*
- You *can / are allowed to ...*

students' rights

- ____________________
- ____________________
- ____________________

teacher's rights

- ____________________
- ____________________
- ____________________

rules for students

- ____________________
- ____________________
- ____________________

rules for teachers

- ____________________
- ____________________
- ____________________

13 Design a flag and coat of arms for your class. Explain why you designed them like this.

flag	coat of arms

14 Now, on a large piece of card, write your Constitution combining the best ideas from the class. Remember that all class members have to sign it.

Skills check

15 Read the text and choose the best word for each space.

The Fathers of the Constitution were seven (1) ____________ leaders who worked together to write the Spanish Constitution in (2) ____________. Even though these leaders came from different political (3) ____________ and had very different political beliefs, they were able to write the Constitution because they had the ability to (4) ____________, respect and understand each other. They also believed in the fundamental values of a democratic society. These values are justice, freedom, equality and respect for difference. The Constitution was approved by (5) ____________ on 31 October 1978 and by the Spanish citizens in a (6) ____________ on 6 December 1978.

1. political / economic / artistic
2. 1987 / 1978 / 1998
3. houses / schools / parties
4. listen / fight / read
5. judges / Parliament / courts
6. referendum / manifesto / campaign

16 Choose the best word to represent your ideas. Compare with a friend.

a. You *mustn't / can / can't* discriminate against people because of their religion.

b. You *should / mustn't / don't have to* vote in elections in Spain.

c. We *have to / don't have to* respect the law.

d. We *have to / don't have to / mustn't* pay taxes.

e. You *have to / can / mustn't* use public transport.

f. Education *is / isn't* a right.

17 Write some rights and responsibilities using the words below.

a. (mustn't) ____

b. (have to) ____

c. (can't) ____

d. (should) ____

UNIT 5 Spanish population

1. Look at the arrows and label the maps.

migrate	emigrate	immigrate

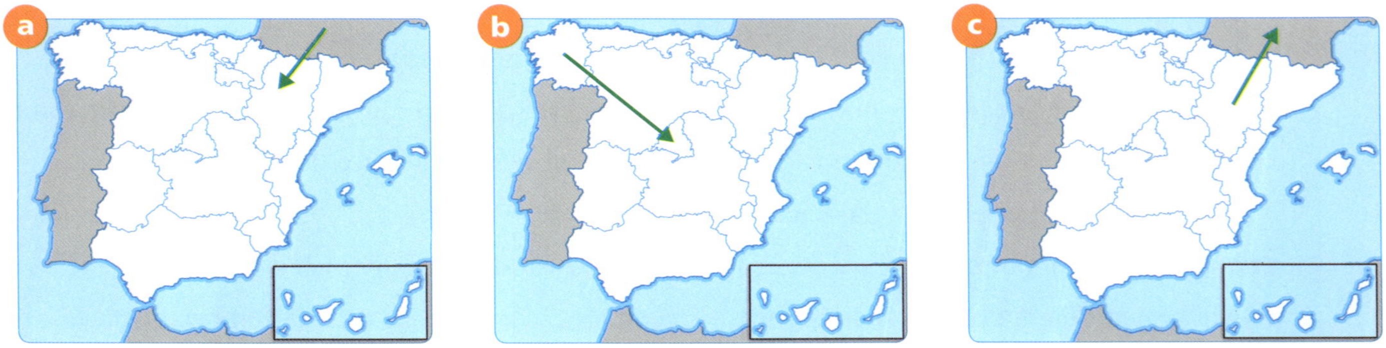

a. ______________________ b. ______________________ c. ______________________

2. Look at the verbs in the box in Activity 1. Change them so they fit the sentences.

a. People who come to Spain from other countries are called i______________ants.

b. If you leave your country, you become an e______________t.

c. Moving from one part of a country to another is called m______________n.

d. M______________y movements are the patterns we talk about when we look at population movements.

e. I______________ion is the action of coming to live in a foreign country.

3. Tick the reasons for population growth. Add two more reasons.

a. better healthcare ☐

b. poverty ☐

c. access to safe drinking water ☐

d. fast food ☐

e. smoking ☐

f. immigration ☐

g. higher hygiene standards ☐

h. illnesses ☐

i. healthy diet ☐

j. vaccination ☐

k. ______________________

l. ______________________

4 Look at the information about three different countries. Which country goes with which data? Why? Calculate the population density for each country and add it to the table.

China	Portugal	The Gambia

	______	______	______
surface area (km²)	92 400	9 600 000	11 300
population	10 600 000	1 400 000 000	1 800 000
life expectancy (years)	79	71	64
number of doctors per 10 000 people	34	14	1
personal computers per 1 000 people	134	17	12
percentage in secondary education	53%	44%	20%
population density	______	______	______

5 Match types of population with their members.

a. child population	**1.** people living in villages
b. adult population	**2.** children, teenagers, retired people
c. elderly population	**3.** people between 15 and 65
d. urban population	**4.** children and teenagers younger than 15
e. rural population	**5.** people living in cities
f. economically active population	**6.** people over 65
g. economically inactive population	**7.** employed people

6 List the groups of population you belong to. Do you belong to the male or female population group?

a. ______________________ **c.** ______________________

b. ______________________ **d.** ______________________

7 Choose the correct words or numbers to complete the text.

In recent years, migration from Spain to other countries has begun to *fall / rise*. Young *single / married* people, aged between *25 / 35* and *35 / 45*, with a high level of education are emigrating to South America and to European countries, such as Germany or the United Kingdom. Many of them go to start *jobs / degrees* in multinational *companies / universities*. At the same time, South Americans continue to migrate to Spain but at a *slower / faster* rate than before.

8 Look at the maps and answer the questions.

a. Which countries did Spaniards emigrate to at the beginning of the 20th century? ______________________

b. Which two cities were the main destinations for internal migration in the 20th century? ______________________

____

c. Which countries did Spaniards emigrate to in the 1970s?

____

____

d. These are some effects of migratory movements. Which map(s) do they refer to?

- overcrowded cities ______________________
- unemployment among rural migrants ______________________
- conflicts between different nationality groups ______________________
- people seen as a cheap labour source ______________________
- loss of young skilled workers ______________________
- cultural diversity ______________________
- abandoned villages ______________________
- culture shock ______________________

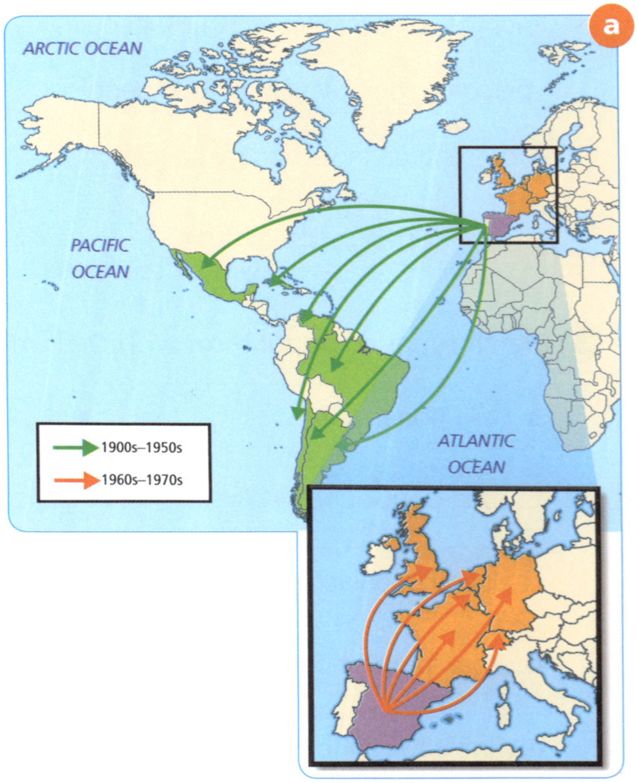

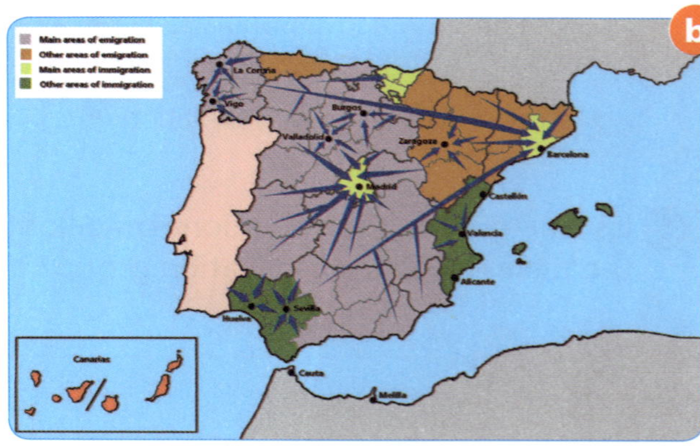

9 What do these numbers refer to? Match.

a. 46 million
b. 1.3
c. 81
d. 93
e. 5 million
f. 35
g. 18 million
h. 4.7
i. 78%

1. number of children per woman in 2014
2. Spain's inhabitants in 1900
3. life expectancy in 2014
4. Spain's population density
5. Spain's inhabitants in 2014
6. immigrants in Spain
7. number of children per woman in 1900
8. life expenctancy in 1900
9. urban population

10 Look at the map and tick the correct sentences.

a. This map shows the distribution of immigrants in Spain. ☐

b. This map shows the distribution of the Spanish population. ☐

c. The province of Cádiz has more inhabitants than the province of Guadalajara. ☐

d. The province of Madrid has more than five million inhabitants. ☐

e. The province of Cuenca has more inhabitants than the province of Huesca. ☐

f. The province of Valencia has more than one millicn inhabitants. ☐

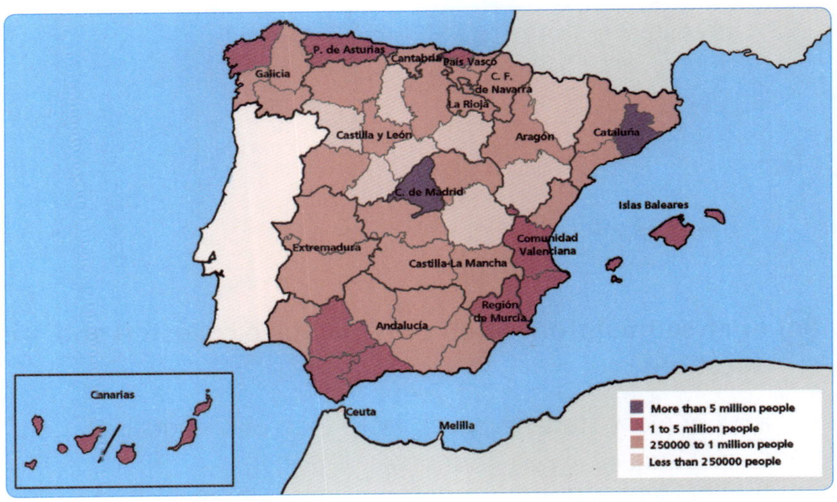

Project work

11 You're going to carry out a census of your class. Write six questions using the categories to help you.

birth date	religion	gender	family	birth place	languages

a. ____________________

b. ____________________

c. ____________________

d. ____________________

e. ____________________

f. ____________________

12 Ask your questions to your classmates. Record the information in your notebook.

13 Choose two categories and present the data. What type of chart will best show the information?

a

b

14 Analyse the information that you have collected and answer the questions.

a. How many students speak more than one language? ____________________

b. What languages do students in your class speak? ____________________

c. Are there more girls or boys in the class? ____________________

d. Where were most of your classmates born? ____________________

Skills check

15 Match the sentences with the corresponding signs. There are four extra sentences.

a. You can't drink this water.
b. You mustn't enter this place with a dog.
c. Only dogs that assist a disabled person can enter.
d. You should drive slowly because there may be children playing near the road.
e. You can put your suitcase near the emergency exit.
f. This water is safe to drink.
g. You mustn't place any items close to the emergency exit.
h. This place is reserved for disabled people.
i. Only people who have a special permit can enter.
j. You can enter without a special permit.

☐ Potable water

☐ No access to unauthorised person

☐ PRIORITY SEAT

☐ CAUTION. CHILDREN PLAYING

☐ FIRE EXIT KEEP CLEAR

☐ No dogs except assistance dogs

16 Read the text and circle the correct words.

The *population distribution / birth rate* of a country often varies in different regions and there are different explanations for this. Firstly, the *temperature / climate* of an area is very important. If the climate is too extreme, it's difficult for *flowers / crops* to grow there and for people to live there. Secondly, the relief of an area can affect the population density. It's difficult to build houses in *mountainous / coastal* areas and transport is often a problem. Finally, economic factors are very important. People will often *migrate to / live in* a place where there are lots of jobs.

17 Write sentences using the words you have chosen in Activity 16.

a. ______________________

b. ______________________

c. ______________________

d. ______________________

e. ______________________

UNIT 6 Europe

1 Look at the photos of famous things from countries in the European Union. Label them with the countries in the box. There are two extra countries.

Italy	Chech Republic	Ireland	Greece	United Kingdom	Netherlands	France	Germany

a

______

b

______

c

______

d

______

e

______

f

______

2 Label the map with the landforms.

1. Loch Ness
2. Tatra Mountains
3. White Cliffs of Dover
4. Plitvice Lakes
5. Mount Etna

3 Search for the information to complete the table. Then calculate the population density of each country.

country	population	surface area (km²)	population density
Sweden			
UK			
Ireland			
Turkey			
Lithuania			
Austria			
Slovakia			
Malta			

4 Look at the map and follow the instructions.

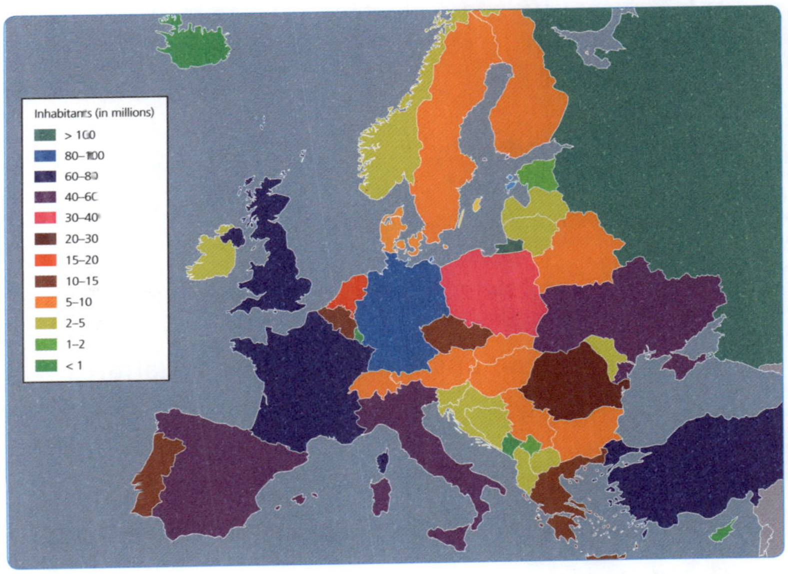

a. List the countries with a population of more than 80 million.

____

b. Which country is more highly populated: Belarus or Belgium?

____

c. List the countries with a population of less than two million.

____

____

d. List the countries with populations larger than 15 million but smaller than 30 million.

____

____

e. Which country has the largest population? _______________

f. Which country has the smallest population? _______________

5 Read about the process of joining the European Union. Fill the gaps with the words from the box.

approved	democratic	administrative	negotiation	applicant	stable

When a new country wants to join the EU, it has to apply to the European Council. The Council bases its decision on the advice of two other institutions: the Commission and the Parliament. The ______________ country must be ______________ and protect human rights. It also has to be economically ______________. It must be ready to adapt its ______________ systems to fit the way the EU works. If the application is accepted, the next stage is ______________ with the other EU member states.

Turkey wants to be in the EU. Its application was ______________ in 1999. Negotiations started in 2005 and have still not finished!

6 Complete the sentences about the EU institutions.

a. The EU's general political direction is decided by the E______________ C______________.

b. European laws and budgets are passed by the E______________ P______________.

c. There are 28 m______________ in the Council and the Commission.

d. EU money is spent by the E______________ C______________.

e. New laws are proposed by the E______________ P______________.

f. Economic and defence policies are set by the C______________ of the ______________.

7 Which EU institutions deal with these situations?

a. A new budget has to be planned.

____

b. An economic agreement will be signed between the EU and Japan.

____

c. One of the members of the EU is not following the law.

____

d. A network of highways is being built in one of the EU member states. The way the money is being spent must be checked. ______________

8. Look at some of the official languages in the EU. Which do you think have the highest number of native speakers? Number them from highest (1) to lowest (8). Then search for the information on the Internet and check your answers.

English ☐	German ☐
Portuguese ☐	Spanish ☐
French ☐	Italian ☐
Romanian ☐	Polish ☐

9. List the rest of the official languages of the EU.

10. Answer the questions.

a. What are three unofficial languages in Europe?

b. Which languages are official in Spain?

c. How do you think the EU decides which languages are official?

11. Research the numbers of speakers of each of the official languages in the EU and draw a graph or pie chart to show the information.

Project work

12 You're going to prepare a quiz about EU countries. Choose five categories from this list or use your own ideas.

national dishes	history	flags	industry	music
physical geography	landmarks	towns or cities		

13 Do some research to help you write 10 questions about different EU countries. Write the questions in the table and the answers in your notebook. Then test the quiz on two classmates.

	classmate 1	classmate 2
What is the largest city in Bulgaria?		

14 Once you've got the results back, look at your quiz again and reflect.

a. Did you make any questions too easy or difficult? Which ones? ____________

b. How can you make the easy questions harder? ____________

c. How can make the difficult questions easier? ____________

d. Give your rewritten quiz to another group. Did they get a different result? ____________

Skills check

15 Read the text about the Alps. Are the sentences below true (T) or false (F)? If there is not enough information, write D (doesn't say).

The Alps are the largest mountain range in Europe. They stretch for more than 1 000 kilometres across France, Italy, Switzerland, Germany, Austria, Slovenia, Lichtenstein and Monaco. The Alps have more than 100 peaks with an altitude of over 4 000 m and Mont Blanc is the highest of them. The Alps form the watershed of many European rivers including the Rhine, the Rhone, the Danube and the Po. The Alps are inhabited by about 14 million people who are distributed across the eight countries. With approximately 120 million tourists a year, the Alps are one of the world's most popular tourist destinations.

a. There are no other European mountain ranges as big as the Alps. ☐

b. The Alps have 200 peaks higher than 4 000 metres. ☐

c. Only four rivers flow from the Alps. ☐

d. The Swiss Alps are also called the Central Alps. ☐

e. The Alps are a very popular holiday destinations. ☐

16 Imagine you have been on holiday in the Alps. Think of things you might say about your trip.

a. how you got there ______

b. who you were with ______

c. how long you stayed ______

d. adjectives for how the Alps looked ______

______

e. how long you stayed ______

17 Your penfriend has written to you asking about your holiday in the Alps. Write back telling him or her about it.

Dear ______

______

______

______

UNIT 7 The Middle Ages

1. Complete the text about the Visigoths using the words from the box. There are two extra words.

Muslims	tribe	peasants	Christianity	capital
Roman	councils	nobles	settle	Latin

The Visigoths were a ______________ from the north of Europe. In the 5th century, the Visigoths started to ______________ in Hispania.
The Visigoth society consisted of a king, ______________ and peasants. The nobles were wealthy families, often related to the king, who owned land and had power. The majority of the population were ______________ who worked on the nobles' land for food and a place to live.
To unite the country, the Visigoths adopted some of the ______________ ways of life. They learnt Latin, converted to ______________ and followed Roman laws. They kept their own customs too. The king and the important members of the Visigoth tribe held ______________ to discuss any problems in the kingdom. Toledo became the ______________ of the Visigoth kingdom. The Visigoths controlled Spain for more than two hundred years.

2. Look at the picture of an Al-Andalus city. Complete the sentences and label the picture.

a. The cities were surrounded by a ______________ for protection.

b. People practised their religion in the ______________.

c. People bought and sold products in the ______________.

d. The royal palace was called the ______________.

e. The ______________ was where the crasftspeople lived.

f. The fort was also called ______________.

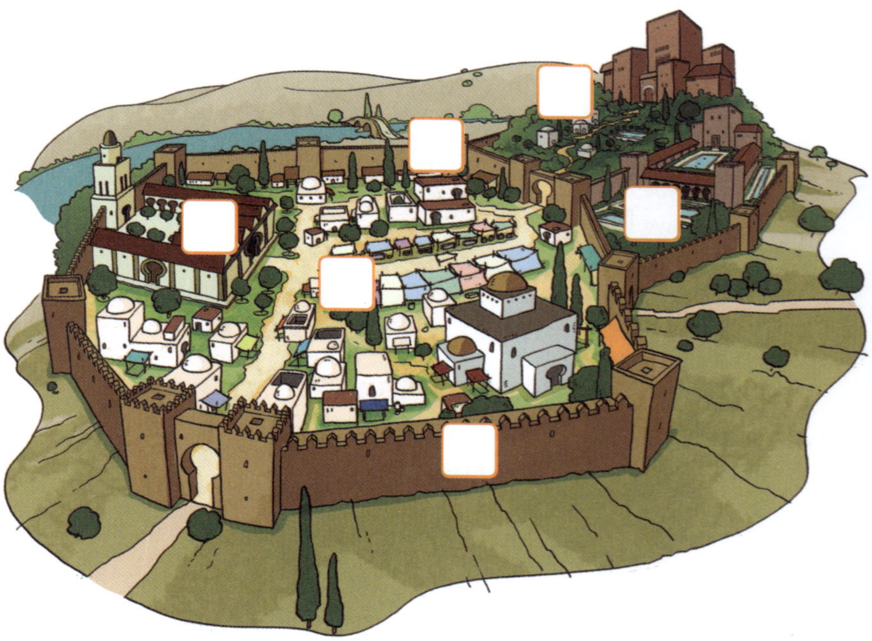

③ **The Muslims contributed many things to Spain. Identify the things in the photos.**

hospital	rice	water wheel	library
Arabic numerals	astrolabe	paper	compass

a

____

b

____

c

____

d

____

e

____

f

____

g

____

h
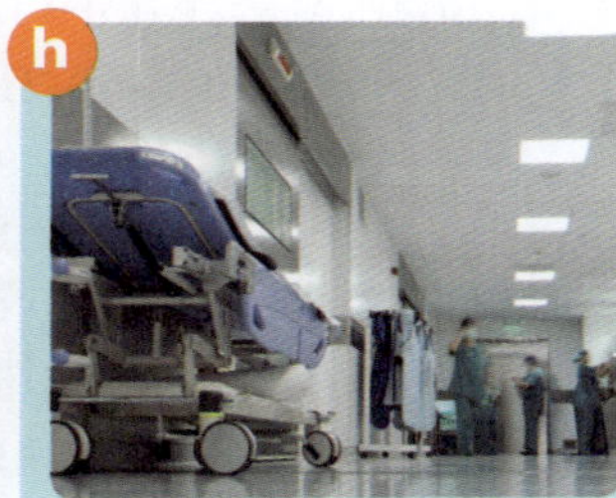
____

④ **Complete the information about the legacy of Al-Andalus using the words from Activity 3.**

The people of Al-Andalus introduced ...

a. ______________ which was used to irrigate crops.

b. ______________ which was used to make books.

c. ______________ which was used to navigate.

d. ______________ which were places dedicated to curing sick people.

e. ______________ which were used to educate and inform people.

f. ______________ which was a new crop for Spain.

g. ______________ which included the important number zero.

h. ______________ which became important in later voyages of discovery.

5 **Read the text about the Reconquista. Write the dates and put the sentences into chronological order.**

a. The Catholic Monarchs defeated the Muslims in Granada. ______ ☐

b. Isabel I of Castilla and Fernando II of Aragón married. ______ ☐

c. Don Pelayo defeated the Muslim army at the Battle of Covadonga. ______ ☐

d. The Muslim army defeated the Visigoths at the Battle of Guadalete. ______ ☐

e. The Christian armies defeated the Muslim army at the Battle of Las Navas de Tolosa. ______ ☐

f. Alfonso VI conquered Toledo. ______ ☐

6 **Read the text about Boabdil, the last ruler of Muslim Spain and complete the sentences about his life.**

Boabdil was born in the Alhambra Palace in Granada in 1460. His nickname was *el Rey Chico*, not because he was small but because his kingdom was getting smaller and smaller as the Christian armies conquered more Muslim territories. Boabdil came to the throne in 1482. Although he was already at war with his own uncle and father, he decided to invade Castilla as well. In 1483, Boabdil was captured and imprisoned in the castle of Lucena. Three years later, in exchange for his liberty, Boabdil agreed to his kingdom paying taxes to the Catholic Monarchs. There were many wars during the next six years and finally the Christian forces placed Granada under siege. The city fell on 2 January 1492. Boabdil was expelled from the city and he and his family and court went to the Alpujarras to live in exile; however, he stayed there for less than a year. Boabdil travelled to Fez in Morocco where he died in 1527. His followers remained in the Alpujarras until they were expelled in 1570.

a. In 1460 ______.

b. In 1482 ______.

c. In 1483 ______.

d. In 1486 ______.

e. On 2 January 1492 ______.

f. In 1527 ______.

g. In 1570 ______.

7 Label the people in a feudal society.

a

____

b

____

c

____

d

____

e

____

8 **Identify the people described below. Then list them in order of their power and influence in feudal society from highest (1) to lowest (6).**

a. They worked on lands governed by nobles, knights or the king. They were free to leave the land. They gave their crops as tax. In return for this tax, the knights and nobles protected them at times of war.

_______________ ☐

b. He owned all the land in his kingdom and made the laws. _______________ ☐

c. They couldn't leave the land where they worked. They were at the bottom of the feudal system, below the peasants even. _______________ ☐

d. They received land from the nobles. In return, they fought in battles for the king. _______________ ☐

e. They received land from the king and in return they protected him and gave him knights for his armies.

_______________ ☐

f. They were Christian religious people such as priests, monks and nuns. _______________ ☐

9 **Classify the words according to the architectural style. Write I for Islamic, R for Romanesque or G for Gothic.**

1. rose windows ☐
2. open courtyards ☐
3. thick walls ☐
4. thin walls ☐
5. horseshoe arches ☐
6. dark inside ☐
7. bright colours ☐
8. small windows ☐
9. pointed arches ☐

Project work

10 Imagine you live in the Middle Ages. Choose one period and think of the various aspects of life. Complete the table. Use the Internet to find the necessary information.

	period: ____________
1. What social or religious group do you belong to?	____________
2. What does the city where you live look like?	____________
3. What styles of architecture can you see in your city?	____________
4. What does your house look like?	____________
5. What type of food do you eat?	____________
6. What clothes do you wear?	____________
7. How do you spend your free time?	____________

11 Write about what your life looks like. Use the information from Activity 10.

I live in ____________

____

____

____

____

____

____

12 Compare your text with your classmate. Did you choose the same period?

Skills check

13 Read the text about castles and match the headings to the correct paragraphs. There are two extra headings.

Hunting | Knights | Tournaments | Castle life | Function of a castle | Entertainment | Food

____

Life in a castle wasn't very comfortable. The rooms were dark and the tapestries on the walls and the straw-covered floors didn't do much to keep the occupants warm. The nobles that lived there often shared the same bedroom, which was a problem because they didn't wash very often!

____

In times of peace, the nobles often organised banquets. The guests ate many different types of food and there was plenty of meat, fish and exotic dishes such as swan. Musicians, acrobats and jesters entertained the guests. Sometimes a travelling singer called a troubadour came to the castle to sing and share news from other regions.

____

The knights had to practise fighting and often had competitions, which they called tournaments. A popular event was jousting. Two knights tried to push each other off their horses using a long, heavy pole called a lance.

____

The nobles often went hunting. They used a bow and arrow to hunt deer and wild pigs in the forests. They also used trained birds of prey to hunt smaller animals. The ladies of the court also practised this sport.

____

The castle served as a home for the nobles and their families as well as the centre of local power. It was a court of law and also a prison.

14 Fill in the gaps to complete the letter.

Dear Lucy,

I'm standing __________ the top of the castle battlements. I can __________ the sea and the mountains from here. It __________ a beautiful place. I came here two days __________ with my class. __________ are many interesting places to visit. Yesterday we went __________ a medieval walled town and walked __________ the walls. I took lots __________ photos. Tomorrow, we are __________ to the beach for the day. The weather is perfect. It's sunny __________ not too hot.

See you __________ Monday.

Love,

Jill

Spain in the 15th and 16th centuries

1 Classify the words according to the period they belong to.

Christopher Columbus   Christian Kingdoms   Al-Andalus   colonisation of America
Don Pelayo   Carlos I   Caliphate of Córdoba   Battle of Lepanto

the Middle Ages	the Early Modern Age
______	______
______	______
______	______
______	______

2 Tick the events that took place in 1492.

a. the conquest of the Kingdom of Granada ☐

b. the marriage of Isabel I of Castilla and Fernando II of Aragón ☐

c. the discovery of America ☐

d. the conquest of Toledo ☐

e. the expulsion of the Jews ☐

f. the expulsion of the Moriscos ☐

g. the publication of the first Spanish grammar book ☐

h. the Battle of Lepanto ☐

i. the end of the Reconquista ☐

3 Complete the text about Columbus' first voyage. Use the words from the box.

America   navigator   Pinta   sea   San Salvador
west   three   Africa   continent   Asia

A ______ called Christopher Columbus wanted to find a new ______ route to Asia. At that time, other navigators sailed around the coast of ______, but Columbus decided to sail ______ across the Atlantic Ocean. The Catholic Monarchs gave him money for this voyage. Three ships, the Santa María, the ______ and the Niña, left Palos de la Frontera on 3 August 1492 and arrived in ______, an island in the Bahamas, on 12 October. Columbus had reached ______, but he thought he had reached ______. Although he made ______ more voyages, he died not knowing that he had discovered a new ______.

4 Answer the questions about the discovery of America.
If necessary, search for the information on the Internet.

a. Why did European monarchs want to find new sea routes to reach Asia?

____

b. Why do you think Isabel I and Fernando II paid for the voyage?

____

c. What problems do you think the sailors had during the voyage?

____

d. Why did Columbus call the inhabitants of America *Indians*?

____

5 Make a list of goods imported from America and a list of goods exported to America. Use the words in the box.

tomatoes cattle wheat corn grapes honeybees pumpkins silver vanilla coffee beans cocoa beans potatoes onions pineapples horses gold rice

import	export

6 Label the photos with the words from Activity 5.

a

____

b

____

c

____

d

____

7 The colonisation of America had both positive and negative effects. Match the words to the explanations.

- **a.** commercial expansion
- **b.** racism
- **c.** exploitation of natural resources
- **d.** new products
- **e.** slavery
- **f.** cross-cultural relations
- **g.** culture and religion
- **h.** disease

1. New viruses from Europe attacked living things on the continent.
2. Tomatoes, potatoes and chocolate arrived in Europe.
3. The Spanish invaders wanted to convert the indigenous population to Christianity and impose the Spanish language.
4. The indigenous people were used as a workforce and were treated badly.
5. Different cultures enriched each other when they came into contact.
6. The Spanish colonisers transported people from the African continent to work.
7. New markets were opened, where people could buy and sell.
8. Precious metals were taken from the indigenous people and sent to Europe.

8 Circle the correct words.

- **a.** Carlos I was the grandson of *the Catholic Monarchs / Felipe II / Don Pelayo*.
- **b.** During his reign, Spain conquered most of *Asia / Africa / America*.
- **c.** Carlos I was also the Holy Roman Emperor and was called Carlos *III / IV / V* of Germany.
- **d.** Carlos I divided the Spanish Empire into *two / three* parts.
- **e.** Felipe II inherited the *Spanish / German* Empire.
- **f.** In 1571 Felipe II defeated the *Turkish / German* Empire.
- **g.** Felipe II conquered *France / Portugal / Italy* in 1580.

9 Which monarchs do the sentences refer to? Write **C** for Carlos I or **F** for Felipe II.

a. His personal motto was *Plus Ultra*. ☐

b. He established the Royal Court in Madrid. ☐

c. He won the Battle of Lepanto. ☐

d. He conquered Portugal. ☐

e. He inherited Spain and its territories from his grandparents. ☐

f. His father gave him Spain and the Netherlands. ☐

10 What happened in these years? Write the sentences.

a. In 1479 ______

b. In 1492 ______

c. In 1516 ______

d. In 1571 ______

e. In 1580 ______

11 Read the text about the Spanish Armada. Decide if the sentences below are true (**T**) or false (**F**).

Felipe II of Spain declared war on England because Elizabeth I would not punish British sailors for attacking Spanish ships returning from America. These sailors were stealing the gold and silver being transported from America to Spain. Felipe II also wanted to convert Protestant England back to Catholicism.

Felipe II's plan was to send 130 Spanish ships with 30 000 soldiers to attack the English fleet and invade England. However, in 1587, the Spanish fleet was destroyed in Cádiz before reaching England. Felipe II built a new fleet, the Armada, which set sail for England in 1588. While anchored near Calais, France, the Armada was attacked by the English, who chased the Spanish ships into the rough North Sea. Here, the heavy Spanish ships were difficult to control and the wind and storms drove them on to the rocks. The Armada lost half its ships and 20 000 soldiers and sailors.

a. The causes of the war were economic and religious. ☐

b. The king of Spain wanted to invade England using more than 100 ships. ☐

c. Felipe II had to rebuild his fleet because the ships had been destroyed when coming back from America. ☐

d. The Armada escaped to Calais. ☐

e. The Spanish ships were difficult to control because of their size and weight. ☐

Project work

12 Search for information about the three pre-Columbian civilisations. Then complete the table.

	the Aztecs	the Mayas	the Incas
time			
language			
location	*Central Mexico*		
main city	*Tenochtitlan*		
government	*governed by an emperor*		
religion	*many gods; temples*		
society			
entertainment			
Science			
art			

13 Choose one civilisation and write a short text about it.

The ______ lived in the region that is known today as ______

Skills check

14 Read about the Aztec civilisation and match the headings to the correct paragraphs. There are two extra headings.

Religion	Diet	Ball game	Sports	Location	Chocolate	Farming	Corn

____

The Aztecs lived in the region that is known today as Central Mexico. The sacred capital of the Aztec empire was called Tenochtitlan. They were governed by an emperor.

____

The Aztecs were farmers who grew many different crops and raised livestock. The farmers raised turkeys and ducks for meat. The most important crop for the Aztecs was corn or maize.

____

The corn was ground between two stones to produce flour, and this flour was used to make a type of flat bread called *tortillas*. The Aztecs ate corn with every meal. In addition, they ate tomatoes, beans, peppers, peanuts and avocados.

____

In Aztec society, privileged people drank a bitter chocolate drink made from cocoa beans. This chocolate drink was not like the chocolate drinks of today. The Aztecs included vanilla, pepper and chilli in their recipe.

____

The Aztecs loved sports. The most popular and probably the most dangerous game involved a rubber ball. The aim of the game was simple: each team tried to get the ball into the opponents' side of the court. Points were also awarded for passing the ball through hoops high above the court. In the Flying Bird game, players wore eagle costumes. The players climbed a high pole and held on to a rope with their legs. They would then swing upside down around the pole. Points were given for speed and style.

____

The Aztecs worshiped many gods. To honour their gods, they built temples in the shape of pyramids. One of the most important gods was the Sun. The Aztecs called themselves the People of the Sun and performed rituals and sacrifices to give the Sun strength.

15 Write the words for the definitions. You will find all the words in the text in Activity 14.

a. ________________: a building with a square base and sloping sides meeting in one point.

b. ________________: a ruler of an empire.

c. ________________: a set of actions preformed regularly, especially as part of a ceremony.

d. ________________: a natural substance used to give flavour to sweet foods, such as ice cream.

Spain in the 17th and 18th centuries

1 Label the social classes in Early Modern Spain. Write **P** for privileged class or **U** for unprivileged class.

a

______________________ ☐

b

______________________ ☐

c

______________________ ☐

d

______________________ ☐

2 Correct the sentences about the end of the Habsburg dynasty in Spain.

a. In the 17th century, Spain was involved in the Thirteen Years' War.

____

b. The Spanish population increased due to wars, plagues and poor harvest.

____

c. The last Bourbon kings left their power in the hands of *validos*.

____

d. The Spanish War of Succession lasted from 1701 to 1710.

____

e. The war ended with the signing of the Treaty of Paris.

____

3 Tick the characteristics of 17th-century Spain.

a. sewage systems ☐
b. *validos* ☐
c. population increase ☐
d. Habsburgs ☐
e. museums ☐
f. street lighting ☐
g. hospitals ☐
h. pavements ☐
i. Bourbons ☐

4. Put the kings in chronological order (1–9) and write the dynasty they belong to. You can look back at Unit 8.

a. Fernando VI ☐ ____________

b. Felipe III ☐ ____________

c. Carlos II ☐ ____________

d. Carlos IV ☐ ____________

e. Felipe II ☐ ____________

f. Felipe V ☐ ____________

g. Carlos III ☐ ____________

h. Felipe IV ☐ ____________

i. Carlos I [1] Habsburg

5. Use the information from Activity 4 to make a timeline.

Carlos I ____________ ____________ ____________ ____________

____________ ____________ ____________ ____________

6. Did the following events take place in the 17th or 18th century?

a. The Thirty Years' War took place. 17th century

b. Many plagues broke out. ____________

c. Cities became more hygienic and safer. ____________

d. Felipe II was king. ____________

e. *Validos* controlled Spain. ____________

f. The Moriscos were expelled from Spain. ____________

g. Many people migrated from Spain to America. ____________

h. The War of Succession took place. ____________

i. Harvests were very poor. ____________

j. Many scientific discoveries were made. ____________

k. The population increased. ____________

l. Felipe V was king. ____________

UNIT 9

7 Write the names of the Baroque painters and writers in the correct column of the table.

Velázquez Cervantes Murillo Lope de Vega Quevedo Góngora
Tirso de Molina Baltasar Gracián Zurbarán Calderón de la Barca

painting	theatre	poetry	novels

8 The main styles of the Golden Age were the Renaissance and Baroque. Read and write **R** for Renaissance or **B** for Baroque.

a. El Greco ☐
b. action and movement ☐
c. Velázquez ☐
d. harmony ☐
e. San Lorenzo de El Escorial ☐
f. Quevedo ☐
g. 15th and 16th centuries ☐
h. Teresa de Ávila ☐
i. 17th and 18th centuries ☐
j. Zurbarán ☐

9 Complete the sentences.

a. The E__________ was a period that brought significant changes to some European countries in the 18th century.
b. In Spain, this period coincided with the reign of F__________ and his successors: Fernando VI, Carlos III and C__________.
c. Education was very i__________ and scientists made great discoveries during this time.
d. One of these scientists was Isaac N__________.
e. The main idea of the Enlightenment was a belief in human r__________ over religion.

10 Read the description and find the people in the painting.

In the centre of the painting we can see Infanta Margarita. She is wearing a long white dress. There are two girls next to the Infanta who are looking after her. They are called *las meninas* (maids of honour). In the foreground on the right there are two dwarves and a large dog. On the left of the painting we can see the artist, Diego Velázquez. He is painting a portrait of the king and queen, Felipe IV and Mariana of Austria. This painting is very interesting because it is composed from the king and queen's point of view. The Infanta and the other people are looking at us and we can see their reflection in the mirror at the back of the room.

a. ____________________

b. ____________________

c. ____________________

d. ____________________

e. ____________________

11 Write a description of the painting *Beggar Boys Eating Grapes and Melon* by Murillo.

Useful expressions

- In the centre ...
- In the foreground ...
- In the background ...
- He is wearing ...
- He is eating ...

____

____

____

____

____

Project work

12 Spain suffered many problems in the 17th century, but conditions seemed to improve in the 18th century. Number the events according to the importance you think they had for society (**1**: the most important; **8**: the least important).

a

Spain in the 17th century	
Spain was involved in many wars over territory and religion.	
There were poor harvests which caused famine.	
There were outbreaks of plagues.	
The Moriscos were expelled from Spain.	
The amount of gold and silver imported from America decreased.	
Spain lost many important territories.	
Administration of the country was in the hands of the king's *validos*.	
People emigrated from Spain to America.	

b

Spain in the 18th century	
The Bourbon dynasty replaced the Habsburg dynasty.	
The Spanish economy improved.	
Many people moved into the towns and cities.	
Carlos III and Carlos IV modernised Spain.	
Cities became safer and more hygienic.	
It was the period of the Enlightenment.	
There were many important scientific discoveries and inventions.	
Industry, agriculture and trade developed.	

13 Choose the most important event from each century. Explain why each event had such a large impact on society.

Scientific discoveries and inventions influenced society because ...

There were many important scientific discoveries and inventions. As a result,...

a. ______________________________

____

____

b. ______________________________

____

____

Skills check

14 Match the sentences with the corresponding signs. There are three extra sentences.

a. You mustn't take bags into the museum.

b. *Las Meninas* is in the permanent exhibition.

c. Children can't visit the museum.

d. Lunch is served all day.

e. It is cheaper for children to visit the museum.

f. You should visit the temporary exhibit today if you want to see *Las Meninas*.

g. You can eat lunch in the Goya Restaurant.

h. You mustn't take photos.

☐ No photos

☐ *Leave your bags here*

☐ TEMPORARY EXHIBIT
LAS MENINAS
LAST DAY TODAY!

☐ ADULTS 8.50 €
CHILDREN 5.00 €

☐ Goya Restaurant
Lunches: 14.00–16.30

15 Read the definitions and write the words.

a. ______________ (*verb*): make better.

b. ______________ (*noun*): a disease that kills a lot of people and spreads very quickly.

c. ______________ (*noun*): the collection of agricultural produce at the end of the growing season.

d. ______________ (*noun*): series of monarchs from the same family.

e. ______________ (*noun*): agreement between two or more states.

f. ______________ (*noun*): person who has the legal right to someone's position or property after they die.

g. ______________ (*verb*): win a victory over an enemy.

h. ______________ (*noun*): system of underground pipes that collects dirty water and waste.

i. ______________ (*noun*): to make someone leave.

16 Write three sentences using three words from Activity 15.

a. ______________________________

b. ______________________________

c. ______________________________

Glossary

English	Your language	English	Your language

Unit 1: The Universe

English	Your language
anticlockwise (adj)	
asteroid (n)	
axis (n)	
burn (v)	
comet (n)	
constellation (n)	
dwarf planet (n)	
eclipse (n)	
elliptical (adj)	
equinox (n)	
erode (v)	
first quarter (n)	
full moon (n)	
galaxy (n)	
galaxy cluster (n)	
gas giant (n)	
hydrogen (n)	
last quarter (n)	
launch (v)	
luminosity (n)	
meteor (n)	
meteorite (n)	
meteoroid (n)	
moon (n)	
new moon (n)	
nucleus (n)	
orbit (n)	
orbit (v)	
reflect (v)	
revolver (v)	
rocky (adj)	
rotate (v)	
solstice (n)	
space debris (n)	
space station (n)	
star (n)	
surface (n)	
tide (n)	
tilted (adj)	

English	Your language	English	Your language

Unit 2: Representing the Earth

English	Your language	English	Your language
accurate (adj)		key (n)	
atmosphere (n)		landmark (n)	
biosphere (n)		landscape (n)	
border (n)		latitude (n)	
carbon dioxide (n)		location (n)	
		longitude (n)	
cardinal points (n)		mantle (n)	
		measure (v)	
cartography (n)		meridian (n)	
compass (n)		network (n)	
compass rose (n)		nitrogen (n)	
		parallel (n)	
core (n)		physical map (n)	
crust (n)			
depth (n)		political map (n)	
device (n)			
distorted (adj)		pressure (n)	
geosphere (n)		scale (n)	
globe (n)		solidify (v)	
grid (n)		three-dimensional (adj)	
height (n)		two-dimensional (adj)	
hemisphere (n)		ultraviolet (adj)	
hydrosphere (n)		weather map (n)	
iron (n)			

Glossary

English	Your language	English	Your language

Unit 3: Climate and weather

English	Your language
alpine climate (n)	
anemometer (n)	
atmospheric pressure (n)	
barometer (n)	
beech (n)	
chamois (n)	
climate graph (n)	
continental climate (n)	
degree (n)	
desert climate (n)	
drought (n)	
equatorial climate (n)	
flood (n)	
global warming (n)	
greenhouse effect (n)	
hare (n)	
harvest (v)	
heat (n)	
heat (v)	
heather (n)	
humidity (n)	
hygrometer (n)	
inland (adj)	
landform (n)	
Mediterranean climate (n)	
meteorologist (n)	
oceanic climate (n)	
polar climate (n)	
rain gauge (n)	
subtropical climate (n)	
thyme (n)	
tropical climate (n)	
trout (n)	
vulture (n)	
weather forecast (n)	

Unit 4: Spain's politics and culture

English	Your language
anthem (n)	
approve (v)	
ballot box (n)	
belief (n)	
campaign (n)	
canditate (n)	
citizen (n)	
coat of arms (n)	
councillor (n)	
court (n)	
cuisine (n)	
define (v)	
democracy (n)	
deputy (n)	
discriminate (v)	
diversity (n)	
elect (v)	
elections (n)	
envelope (n)	
equality (n)	
flag (n)	
forbidden (adj)	
freedom (n)	
government (n)	
healthcare (n)	
heir (n)	
heritage (n)	
ingredient (n)	
judge (n)	
justice (n)	
law (n)	
leader (n)	
member (n)	
participate (v)	
patron saint (n)	
political party (n)	
Prime Minister (n)	
respect (v)	
rights (n)	
senator (n)	
sentence (n)	
speech (n)	
tax (n)	
territory (n)	
tolerate (v)	
tribunal (n)	
vote (v)	

Glossary

English	Your language

Unit 5: Spanish population

English	Your language
abandon (n)	
abandoned (adj)	
actual increase (n)	
add (v)	
advantage (n)	
available (adj)	
be born (v)	
birth (n)	
census (n)	
consequence (n)	
death (n)	
decrease (v)	
demography (n)	
die (v)	
disadvantage (n)	
divide (v)	
elderly (adj)	
emigration (n)	
factory (n)	
immigration (n)	
increase (v)	
inhabitant (n)	
measurement (n)	
natural increase (n)	
opportunity (n)	
overcrowded (adj)	
pollution (n)	
populated (adj)	
population (n)	
population density (n)	
population pyramid (n)	
poverty (n)	
quality of life (n)	
rural (adj)	
rural exodus (n)	
size (n)	
statistics (n)	
subtract (v)	
supply (n)	
survey (n)	
unemployment (n)	
urban (adj)	
vary (v)	

Unit 6: Europe

English	Your language
adopt (v)	
age (n)	
age (v)	
agreement (v)	
arrival (n)	
audit (v)	
average (adj)	
banknote (n)	
benefit (n)	
budget (n)	
coal (n)	
coin (n)	
complaint (n)	
conflict (n)	
cover (v)	
currency (n)	
develop (v)	
diplomatic (adj)	
dispute (n)	
ensure (v)	
freely (adj)	
fund (n)	
heavy machinery (n)	

English	Your language
initiative (n)	
motto (n)	
mountain chain (n)	
multicultural (adj)	
number plate (n)	
peak (n)	
pension (n)	
plain (n)	
policy (n)	
promote (v)	
proposal (n)	
prosperous (adj)	
protect (v)	
public-spirited (adj)	
purpose (n)	
refuse (v)	
represent (v)	
security (n)	
share (v)	
strengthen (v)	
stretch (v)	
treaty (n)	
value (n)	
war (n)	

Glossary

English	Your language	English	Your language

Unit 7: The Middle Ages

English	Your language	English	Your language
Arabic numerals (n)	______	kingdom (n)	______
	______	knight (n)	______
aubergine (n)	______	knowledge (n)	______
battle (n)	______	marry (v)	______
caliph (n)	______	megalith (n)	______
cave painting (n)	______	merchant (n)	______
	______	monk (n)	______
clergy (n)	______	noble (n)	______
conquer (v)	______	nomad (n)	______
conquest (n)	______	nun (n)	______
convert (v)	______	peasant (n)	______
courtyard (n)	______	pilgrimage (n)	______
craft (n)	______	proclaim (v)	______
custom (n)	______	relative (n)	______
defeat (v)	______	rose window (n)	______
discuss (v)	______	rule (v)	______
dome (n)	______	serf (n)	______
feudalism (n)	______	settle (v)	______
fight (v)	______	stained glass (n)	______
guild (n)	______	tomb (n)	______
horseshoe arch (n)	______	treasure (n)	______
	______	tribe (n)	______
invade (v)	______	victory (n)	______
irrigation (n)	______	wealthy (adj)	______

English	Your language	English	Your language

Unit 8: Spain in the 15th and 16th centuries

English	Your language	English	Your language
alliance (n)		native (adj)	
caravel (n)		nutmeg (n)	
city-state (n)		onion (n)	
contribution (n)		passage (n)	
convinced (adj)		permanent (adj)	
descendant (n)		privilege (n)	
discover (v)		promise (v)	
dynasty (n)		pumpkin (n)	
empire (adj)		punish (v)	
expel (v)		ransom (n)	
explorer (n)		reign (n)	
export (v)		reinforce (v)	
expulsion (n)		Renaissance (n)	
finance (v)		sail (v)	
flour (n)		scholar (n)	
gold (n)		silver (n)	
governor (n)		spice (n)	
honeybee (n)		sponsor (v)	
import (v)		temple (n)	
impose (v)		turkey (n)	
inherit (v)		voyage (n)	
leather (n)		war (n)	
llama (n)		weaken (v)	
mainland (n)		wool (n)	

Glossary

English	Your language	English	Your language

Unit 9: Spain in the 17th and 18th centuries

English	Your language	English	Your language
balance (n)		painter (n)	
Baroque (n)		painting (n)	
bishop (n)		pavement (n)	
coincide (v)		pirate (n)	
contrast (n)		plague (n)	
crisis (n)		poetry (n)	
decline (n)		portrait (n)	
dependence (n)		portray (v)	
distribute (v)		printing press (n)	
elaborate (adj)		privileged (adj)	
Enlightenment (n)		replace (v)	
famine (n)		ruler (n)	
feature (n)		salary (n)	
fountain (n)		sewage (n)	
hierarchical (adj)		shopkeeper (n)	
homeless (adj)		sign (v)	
hygienic (adj)		soldier (n)	
independence (n)		splendour (n)	
influence (n)		still life (n)	
lawyer (n)			
martyr (n)		style (n)	
misery (n)		transmit (v)	
modernise (v)		unprivileged (adj)	
monarch (n)		wealth (n)	